Giochiamo Tutti Insieme

20 games to play with children
to encourage and reinforce
Italian language and vocabulary

Kathy Williams

Brilliant Publications

Published by Brilliant Publications
Sales and despatch:
>BEBC Brilliant Publications
>Albion Close, Parkstone, Poole, Dorset BH12 3LL
>Tel: 0845 1309200   01202 712910
>Fax: 0845 1309300
>e-mail: brilliant@bebc.co.uk
>website: www.brilliantpublications.co.uk

Editorial and marketing:
>Unit 10, Sparrow Hall Farm, Edlesborough, Dunstable,
>Bedfordshire LU6 2ES

The name Brilliant Publications and its logo are registered trade marks.

Written by Kathy Williams
Cover and inside illustrations by Chantel Kees
Copyright © Kathy Williams 2006

ISBN: 978-1-903853-96-2

Printed 2006 in the UK, reprinted 2007
10 9 8 7 6 5 4 3 2

Contents

All the games involve speaking, and most can be adapted to practise alternative language. See individual game descriptions for ideas.

Introduction

The games in this book are designed to complement language teaching and learning, either in the classroom or at home. They are fun to play, and there is no age limit – children and adults alike can enjoy the different types of games.

Each game concentrates on one or two specific language areas. Many of the games can be adapted to practise other language vocabulary as appropriate.

All the games encourage speaking and listening. The skills of reading and writing are emphasized to different degrees in the different games.

The instructions for each game set out:
■	the objectives for the game
■	how to set it up
■	how to play it
■	extensions/variations

Some of the games require cards and boards and these are provided as photocopiable resource pages. It is a good idea to allow some time to prepare the items needed for each game before introducing them into play. If the playing cards and boards are photocopied onto thin card and laminated, you will be able to use them again and again for many years.

Giochiamo Tutti Insieme © Kathy Williams

Buongiorno ball game

Action game

Objectives

- To practise key introduction words
- Game can be extended to include other introduction phrases as required

Setting up the game

- You need two or more different coloured balls.

How to play the game

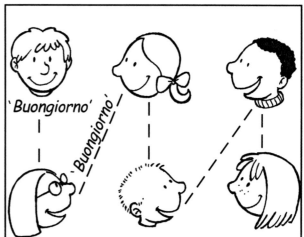

1. Pupils stand in two lines facing each other. The end pupil starts with one of the balls, and throws it to the pupil opposite. That person then throws the ball to the pupil diagonally opposite, who throws it this time to the person directly opposite and so on. The ball thus makes its way in a zig-zag along the two lines.

2. While throwing and catching the ball, each pupil must say 'Buongiorno' or 'Ciao'. Using a different coloured ball, repeat the game, but this time say 'Arrivederci'.

3. Now, tell the children to take note of the colour of the ball. Using the red ball, for instance, they say 'Buongiorno', and with the blue ball they say 'Arrivederci'.

4. Start the game off with one ball again, then introduce the other ball after a couple of throws. This makes them think about which word they are saying! You could introduce further coloured balls with 'Come stai?', 'Sto bene, grazie', 'Mi chiamo …'. Try as many as the group can manage!

5. As a rounding-up test, stand in a large circle, and pick a pupil to hold the coloured balls in the centre. They then throw the balls (gently!) to pupils at random who must say the appropriate phrase for that colour of ball as it is thrown. Younger pupils may find that concentrating on more than two colours/phrases at once is too difficult, but older groups will enjoy the challenge of several colours/phrases in this game.

Extensions/variations

- Adapt the game to practise vocabulary groups; each time a player catches the ball the pupil must say a different animal word/colour/food item.
- Use the ball throwing idea to practise lists of words, passing the ball up and down the line or in a circle; practise the alphabet in Italian/days/months/numbers.

Colour relay

Objective
- To practise saying colour words and respond by picking up the correct colour from a choice

Setting up the game
- Pupils play in teams.
- You will need several items of different colours, the same number of items for each team.
- The game is best played in a large space so that the participants can run back and forth.

Parole importanti – Key words

rosso	red
bianco	white
azzurro	blue
nero	black
verde	green
rosa	pink
giallo	yellow
marrone	brown
arancio	orange
grigio	grey

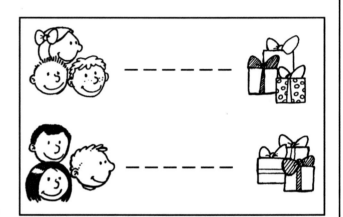

How to play the game
1. Place sets of coloured items in piles at one end of the room (or space you are playing in).
2. The teams line up opposite the coloured items so that they can race against each other in a back-and-forth relay.
3. The teacher calls out the first colour to start the race.
4. The first team member from each team runs to collect that coloured item from their team pile, and returns to the team.
5. On their return they say another colour (in Italian) to be picked up. The next player runs to collect that coloured item, returns to the rest of the team and says the next colour to be picked up.
6. The game continues in this way, with players joining the back of the line on their return to the team, storing all the items at the back of the line, until all the coloured items have been collected.
7. The winning team is the one that successfully collects all the items first. It is a good idea to have three or four small teams, with extra helpers to monitor the teams, so that everyone gets more than one turn, and you can listen carefully to the players saying the colours in ITALIAN. You could have a rule that anyone heard saying the wrong colour, or not using Italian, has to run back and forth again (without picking up another item) before the next player has a turn.

Extension/variation
- To make the game more challenging pupils could say two or three colours at once, with plenty of items in the pile to choose from.

Giochiamo Tutti Insieme © Kathy Williams

Slap down numbers

Objectives
- To practise saying the numbers one to ten
- To listen carefully
- To respond quickly to recognition of numbers in Italian

Parole importanti – Key words

uno	one
due	two
tre	three
quattro	four
cinque	five
sei	six
sette	seven
otto	eight
nove	nine
dieci	ten

Setting up the game
- Players are in pairs, sitting at a table, or where they can put their hands down quickly onto a flat surface.

How to play the game
1. Toss a coin to decide who starts. Both players have their hands on their heads to begin the game.
2. Choose one player to start first. Both players count together in Italian, slowly.
3. When the counting reaches the number that player one has decided to stop at, he slaps his hands down, and spreads out the appropriate number of fingers on the table. For example the counting goes: 'uno ... due ... tre ...' but on 'quattro' he slaps his hand down showing four fingers. Encourage the children to use both hands.
4. Player two must respond as quickly as possible by putting her hands down too, BUT she too must only put down the correct number of fingers, i.e. in this case only four.
5. If she puts the correct number of fingers down, then she becomes the caller. If she is not correct then player one continues to make the number choices.

Extension/variation
- The game can be made more challenging by counting up in twos, by counting backwards or by counting very quickly.

Calling all animals

Objective
- To practise saying animal words

Setting up the game
- Any number of pupils can play. Each player can have a different animal name given to them if there are 10 or less players; if there are more players the animal words can be used more than once.
- You need enough space for the group to form a circle.

Parole importanti – Key words

gatto (m)	cat
topo (m)	mouse
cane (m)	dog
ragno (m)	spider
cavallo (m)	horse
coniglio (m)	rabbit
pesce (m)	fish
uccello (m)	bird
porcellino d'India (m)	guinea-pig
rana (f)	frog

How to play the game
1. The group forms a circle and one pupil is chosen at random to be 'it', in the middle of the circle.
2. All the animal words should be introduced and practised first so that everyone is familiar with the words.
3. Each player is then given an animal name. The whole group hears the names being given out and they can all practise each word as it is introduced. Make sure that everyone knows exactly how to say what they are, and that the person in the middle can say all the animal words (some reminding might be needed).
4. The player who is 'it' decides on an animal name to say and says it aloud three times in succession.
5. The aim of the game is for the person who has been given that animal name to join in and say their name once but before the 'it' person has finished saying it three times! If the 'animal' succeeds, he/she is then 'it' instead. If the 'it' person manages to say the word three times before the person with that animal name has said his name once, the player in the middle stays as 'it'. Everyone who manages to be 'it' must aim to stay there as long as possible, and all the others must try to get him/her out.
6. If the circle players cannot join in before their names are said three times, adjust to saying the name five times (sometimes needed for younger children).

Extensions/variations
- This game is very adaptable as it can be played with any vocabulary that you wish to practise, e.g. buildings, food, parts of the body. It works well with Italian girls'/boys' names.
- Another way to play is for you to spell the animal word out, either in Italian or English. The player who thinks that the animal name is theirs has to run around the outside of the circle back to their place before you finish spelling the word (do it slowly to give them a chance!), and say the word to make sure they were right to run.

Giochiamo Tutti Insieme

Domino months

Objective

- To practise the months in Italian with particular emphasis on word recognition in writing

Setting up the game

- Pupils can either play in pairs or groups with one set of dominoes (page 10) per pair.
- The dominoes could be coloured, decorated, and laminated and/or mounted on card before use.

Parole importanti – Key words

gennaio	January
febbraio	February
marzo	March
aprile	April
maggio	May
giugno	June
luglio	July
agosto	August
settembre	September
ottobre	October
novembre	November
dicembre	December

How to play the game

1. Place the dominoes face down in front of the players with one domino upturned to start the game. The aim of the game is to match the dominoes to make complete month words.

2. Players each take five dominoes at random and look at them without revealing them to their opponent(s). The rest of the dominoes are put in a pile on the table.

3. One player takes a turn first, trying to complete a month word by placing one of his dominoes before or after the starting domino. Dominoes can be placed at right angles so the words do not have to go in one continuous straight line. If the first player cannot go, the other player(s) take their turn. If none of the players can place a domino, then the first player picks one up from the pile and plays the card if it completes a domino month. Play continues with players either putting down a domino or picking one up from the pile.

4. The winner is the player who uses up all of their dominoes first, or who has the least number of cards left. It isn't always possible to carry on until all the dominoes have been put down. In the case of a tie-break, maybe add the number of letters on each card together, the person with the least being the winner!

5. You will need to monitor correct positioning of the dominoes to ensure correct word completion. Saying the names of the months out loud as they are completed helps to link the written and spoken words.

Domino months

bre	novem	bre	lu	bre	giu
bre	dicem	glio	otto	io	settem
bre	a	prile	mar	gno	febbra
io	ma	ggio	lu	sto	genna
io	febbra	gno	otto	io	giu
zo	genna	zo	genna	sto	mar
io	ago	glio	ago	glio	lu

Giochiamo Tutti Insieme

Write back

Objectives

- To reinforce knowledge of numbers up to twenty
- Version 1 practises recognition of number words. Version 2 reinforces the spellings of the numbers

Setting up the game

- Pupils play in pairs using one of the grids from number sheet (page 12) per pair, or one customized in advance to practise specific numbers or words (page 13).
- The children will need some counters or coins.

How to play the game

Version 1

1. The players have a number grid in front of them. Depending on their skill, this can be either A, B or C (from page 12) or one you have custom made using page 13.
2. Player one looks at the grid, decides on a number, but does not tell their partner. Using a finger, player one gently taps out that amount on their partner's back.
3. The partner then places a counter on the correct number on the grid and recites the number in Italian.
4. The game continues with each player taking turns until all the numbers are covered.

Version 2

1. The players have a grid as in version 1, but instead of tapping the required number of times for their partner to recognize, they must slowly spell out the word on their partner's back. It is best to 'draw' one letter at a time, rather than write the whole word in joined-up writing. However, the whole word technique works well with older or more able pupils.
2. As before, the player on whose back the word is written must place their counter on the correct word on the grid, saying it in Italian.

Extension/variation

- This game can be adapted to reinforce spellings in any language area using the blank grid to set out the language to be practised. Alternatively, the 'receiving' player writes down what they think has been spelled on their back onto a blank grid.

Parole importanti – Key words

uno	one
due	two
tre	three
quattro	four
cinque	five
sei	six
sette	seven
otto	eight
nove	nine
dieci	ten
undici	eleven
dodici	twelve
tredici	thirteen
quattordici	fourteen
quindici	fifteen
sedici	sixteen
diciasette	seventeen
diciotto	eighteen
dicianove	nineteen
venti	twenty

Write back number grid

Photocopy one grid per pair (can use either Grid A, B or C)

Grid A

uno	due	tre	quattro	cinque
sei	sette	otto	nove	dieci

Grid B

uno	due	tre	quattro	cinque
sei	sette	otto	nove	dieci
undici	dodici	tredici	quattordici	quindici
sedici	diciasette	diciotto	dicianove	venti

Grid C

undici	dodici	tredici	quattordici	quindici
sedici	diciasette	diciotto	dicianove	venti

Giochiamo Tutti Insieme
© Kathy Williams

Write back blank number grid

Use this to prepare the language that you want to practise, or use the grid to write your answers in.

Grid A

Grid B

Grid C

Rhyming pairs

Objectives

- To facilitate close examination of familiar words in their written form
- Saying the words out loud links the spelling patterns with pronunciation
- To encourage pupils to look closely at the last TWO syllables to find the rhyming pairs, such as '-ese', '-ane', '-ello', as Italian words nearly all end in vowels, so often rhyme easily with many others

Setting up the game

- You need to photocopy and cut out the rhyme cards (pages 15–16).
- The children will need some counters or coins.
- Players play in groups of three. Each pupil will need to pick a picture board from the selection (pages 16–17).

▪▪▪ Parole importanti – Key words

inglese	English
francese	French
madre (f)	mother
padre (m)	father
fratello (m)	brother
uccello (m)	bird
occhio (m)	eye
negozio (m)	shop
pantaloni (m, pl)	trousers
tortelloni (m, pl)	type of pasta
pane (m)	bread
cane (m)	dog
bambino (m)	child
giardino (m)	garden
terrazza (f)	terrace
ragazza (f)	girl
stanza (f)	room
vacanza (f)	holiday

How to play the game

1. All the cards are placed face down and spread out on the table in front of the players.
2. The game is played as a matching pictures pairs game, only this time the matching pairs are rhyming written words.
3. Players must take turns to turn over two cards at random.
4. If they have a rhyming pair they say the two words.
5. If the pair does not rhyme they turn the cards back over and try to remember for next time where each card is.
6. When a player finds a matching pair he/she looks to see if the pair is pictured on their board.
7. If it is, they place counters or coins on the appropriate pictures and put the cards to one side. If the cards aren't pictured, he/she puts them back in the middle of the table, face down.
8. The winner is the player who completes their board first.

Extension/variation

- Players could play the game using boards and words they have created themselves. They could use vocabulary they already know (chosen either individually or as a group) or use dictionaries to look up new words.

Giochiamo Tutti Insieme

Rhyming pairs game cards

inglese	francese
madre	padre
fratello	uccello

occhio	negozio
pantaloni	tortelloni
pane	cane

This page may be photocopied for use by the purchasing institution only.

Giochiamo Tutti Insieme

www.brilliantpublications.co.uk

Rhyming pairs game cards

bambino	giardino
terrazza	ragazza
stanza	vacanza

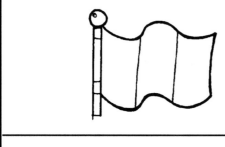 

Giochiamo Tutti Insieme   © Kathy Williams

Rhyming pairs board

Spelling snake

Objective

■ To encourage the use of a specific area of vocabulary or to give players the opportunity to use any language that they know

Setting up the game

■ This game can be played with four or more people.

■ Each child needs a blank copy of the 'spelling snake' (page 20).

How to play the game

1. Start as a whole group and brainstorm a large number of words within a vocabulary area, or several areas. At the end of this session, write these words, correctly spelled onto the board, or provide a prepared list that contains the words you elicited from the players. (This list would benefit from containing words that start or finish with a variety of letters – take care that not all your words end in the letter 'o' for example).

2. Give the players a couple of minutes to study the words, then remove them from view.

3. Each player writes one word of their choice from the target list into the first section of their spelling snake (see 'Cominciare quì').

4. All players then simultaneously pass the snake on to another player, and here you must ensure random exchanges.

5. Using the final letter of the first word, each player must then write in a new word from the list, and then pass the snake on as before.

6. If a player cannot write a word starting with the last letter (which is very often not possible), he/she writes a new word that is unconnected and passes on the snake as before.

7. The class continue to write on and pass around the snakes until all the spaces are full. You can make the game easier by allowing repeats of the same word, or harder by having a 'no repeats' rule.

8. When the snakes are complete, and there may be some which take longer than others, the snake that each player ends with becomes the one which will score or lose them points.

Giochiamo Tutti Insieme

To score points

- Ask each player to check the words on his snake against the original list. A correctly spelled word gets 2 points. Add on an extra 1 point for every word that starts with the last letter of the previous one. The winner is the player with the highest total of points at the end.
- If you tell the players how the scoring works before they start to play it will encourage everyone to spell correctly as they do not know which snake they will have at the end.

Extensions/variations

- Alternatively, tell the players that they are going to be able to use any words they like during the game, but that spelling must be correct. In this case play the game and then include a follow-up session to go over the words and their spellings together.
- If players do not have time to study the words immediately before the game, this game can be used to test spelling knowledge of a preset group of words.

Spelling snake

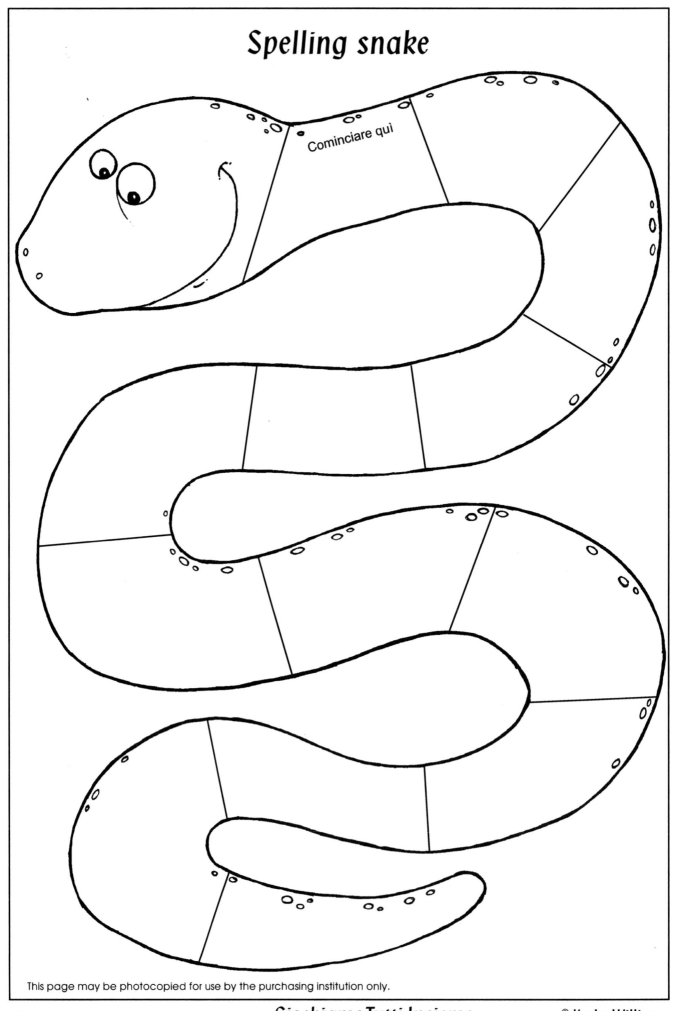

Cominciare qui

Giochiamo Tutti Insieme

Sort yourself out

Objective
- To arrange sets of words beginning with the same letter into alphabetical order

Setting up the game
- You need 'sort yourself out' list of words (page 22) and blank sheets for the children's answers.
- Children will need some scissors and some pens/pencils.
- Children play in pairs.

How to play the game
1. Cut the word lists into separate columns and give each pair of children one list.
2. The children cut the words out individually into strips and mix them up.
3. They then must try to put their words into alphabetical order. They write down the words and their meanings, guessing for those they don't know. You could set a time limit for this task.
4. At the end of the allotted time, the teacher reads out or writes down the correct alphabetical order for each list and the word meanings. Players get a point for every correct position in the list and a point for each correct meaning.

Extension/variation
- The game can be played again using a different set of words or you could create your own list. This game is very useful for checking the pupils' understanding of vocabulary practised.

Parole importanti – Key words

acqua (f)	water
agosto	August
albergo (m)	hotel
albero (m)	tree
amico (m)	friend
arancia (f)	orange
banana (f)	banana
banca (f)	bank
bicchiere (m)	glass
bicicletta (f)	bicycle
buongiorno	hello
burro (m)	butter
camera (f)	room
campo (m)	field
capello (m)	hat
cappuccino (m)	white coffee
città (f)	city
cucina (f)	kitchen
gelato (m)	ice-cream
giallo	yellow
giardino (m)	garden
giorno (m)	day
grande	big
grazie	thank you
madre (f)	mother
mela (f)	apple
mercato (m)	market
mercoledì	Wednesday
museo (m)	museum
musica (f)	music
pane (m)	bread
pantaloni (m,pl)	trousers
pizza (f)	pizza
pizzeria (f)	café-bar
primavera (f)	Spring
prosciutto (m)	ham
quadro (m)	picture
qualcosa	something
quando	when
quanto	how much
quarto (m)	quarter
quattro	four
regalo (m)	present
riso (m)	rice
risotto (m)	risotto
ristorante (m)	restaurant
Roma	Rome
rosa (f)	rose, pink
vacanza (f)	holiday
venerdì	Friday
venti	twenty
vento (m)	wind
verde	green
vino (m)	wine

Sort yourself out

acqua	banana	camera
agosto	banca	campo
albergo	bicchiere	cappello
albero	bicicletta	cappuchino
amico	buongiorno	città
arancia	burro	cucina
gelato	madre	pane
giallo	mela	pantaloni
giardino	mercato	pizza
giorno	mercoledì	pizzeria
grande	museo	primavera
grazie	musica	prosciutto
quadro	regalo	vacanza
qualcosa	riso	venerdì
quando	risotto	venti
quanto	ristorante	vento
quarto	Roma	verde
quattro	rosa	vino

Giochiamo Tutti Insieme

Silly sentences

Objective

- To encourage recognition of sentence building rules and parts of speech

Setting up the game

- Prepare the game by photocopying and cutting out the word sections (page 24), one for every player or pair of players.

How to play the game

1. Give each player (or pair) a set of mixed-up word sections.
2. Discuss the parts of a sentence: noun (il nome), verb (il verbo), adjective (l'adgiettivo - m). Point out that in Italian the adjective usually follows the noun.
3. Demonstrate a sentence that makes sense, for example 'L'agricoltore porta un cappello rosso e verde.'
4. Ask the players to form as many sensible sentences as they can, by changing around the words. Look at and discuss the parts of speech and word order.
5. Ask the pupils to see what 'silly' sentences they can create. Remember that the 'silly' sentences should still be formed correctly, e.g. 'Il cane mangia un capello delizioso.'

Parole importanti – Key words

l'agricoltore	the farmer
il cane	the dog
il gatto	the cat
porta	he/she/it wears
mangia	he/she/it eats
caccia	he/she/it chases
un capello	a hat
un prosciutto	a piece of ham
un pallone	a balloon
rosso	red
verde	green
delizioso	delicious
lungo	long
azzurro	blue

Extension/variation

- Players could draw pictures of their favourite sentences. Play a mime game, where a pupil has to mime what has been drawn and the other players have to guess the 'silly' sentence.

Silly sentences

L'agricoltore | porta | un capello | rosso | e verde

Il cane | mangia | un prosciutto | delizioso

Il gatto | caccia | un pallone | lungo | e azzurro

Giochiamo Tutti Insieme

© Kathy Williams

Wacky meals

Objective

- To recognize and use some food words, as well as the correct words for the different meal times

Setting up the game

- Players are in pairs or small groups.
- Each group will need a set of food word cards (page 27) and a 'menù' (page 28).

How to play the game

1. Each group has a set of food cards face down in front of them.
2. One player picks up a card at random and places it face up in the first 'per la colazione' position on the menu, saying aloud what the food item is in Italian.
3. The second player then picks up another card and places it on the next breakfast position, saying the food item in Italian. Some strange breakfast choices may be beginning to appear!
4. Players continue until all the meals are set.
5. When finished they discuss together what meals have been created using the sentence structures: 'Per la colazione prendo …' And so on.
6. Each pair or group then presents the 'wacky meals' that they have on their menus to the rest of the class.

Parole importanti – Key words

per …	for …
la colazione	breakfast / lunch
il pranzo / la cena	dinner / supper
prendo …	I'm having …
una mela	an apple
del pane	some bread
del burro	some butter
un dolce	a cake
delle carote	some carrots
del formaggio	some cheese
della cioccolata	some chocolate
una insalata	a salad
dei piselli	some peas
del salame	some salami
un caffè	a coffee
una pizza	a pizza
del coca	some coke
delle tagliatelle	some pasta ribbons
del prosciutto crudo	some ham
un tè	a tea
un acqua minerale	a mineral water
delle patate fritte	some chips

Extensions/variations

- The picture cards (page 26) can be used instead of the food word cards to prompt usage of food words.
- The game can be played as a whole class if the menu sheet is enlarged. Individuals take turns to choose cards and place them or write the food item onto the menu.
- Using the same concept, make cards showing different items of clothing, and instead of a menu sheet, use places/events to dress for, for example 'Per andare **in vacanza** porto … (To go **on holiday** I wear …); Per andare **a la scuola** porto … (To go **to school** I wear …); Per andare **a una festa** porto … (To go **to a party** I wear …).' See what funny outfits emerge!

Wacky meals picture cards

Giochiamo Tutti Insieme

© Kathy Williams

✂

una mela	del pane	del burro
un dolce	delle carote	del formaggio
della cioccolata	una insalata	dei piselli
del salame	un caffè	una pizza
del coca	delle tagliatelle	del prosciutto crudo
un tè	un acqua minerale	delle patate fritte

Wacky meals menu sheet

Menu choices

1 Per la colazione	2	3
1 Per il pranzo	2	3
1 Per la cena	2	3

Giochiamo Tutti Insieme

House designers

Objectives
- To use the names for rooms in the house
- To communicate information about the layout of a house
- The use of 'quì' (here), 'lì' (there) and 'è' (is) can also be reinforced

Setting up the game
- Pupils play in teams of three, with the teams racing each other.
- Two 'house design sheets' (page 30) are needed per group. Room pictures (page 31) can be used for guidance.
- A spacious room/area (two rooms could be used) to separate two of the three players in each team, so that they cannot see the other player's sheet.

Parole importanti – Key words

questo quì	this one (here)
lì	there
è	is
la cucina	the kitchen
il salotto	the lounge
la camera da letto	the bedroom
l'ingresso	the hall
la stanza da bagno / il bagno	the bathroom
il garage	the garage
la sala da pranzo	the dining room
la soffitta	the attic

How to play the game

1. One pair of players (players two and three) has a 'house design sheet', a set of room pictures, and a pen/pencil, and sits some distance away from their other team-mate, or in another room.

2. Player one in the team has a 'house design sheet' and a pen/pencil.

3. Player one starts the game by deciding which room to designate first. For example, if he/she decides that the upstairs room on the right is the bedroom, he/she writes 'la camera da letto' or draws a picture of a bed inside that room.

4. When all the player ones from each competing team have made their decision the teacher tells the player twos to start.

5. Player two from each team visits his/her team-mate to find out which room has been chosen, while player three remains behind with a blank 'house design sheet'. On his return, player two tells player three what and where the room is on their design sheet, **in Italian, not in English!** For example, in this case, they will need to point to the upstairs right room and say 'questo quì è la camera da letto'. Player three must then write in the words 'la camera da letto', or draw an appropriate picture, in the correct room.

6. In the meantime player one chooses another room. Player two returns to player one to find out the whereabouts of the next room and returns to player three to relay that piece of information.

7. The winning team is the one who is first in relaying all the information correctly. Remind players that all of the information should be spoken in Italian, and although a picture may be drawn instead, this will only take up extra time.

© Kathy Williams   *Giochiamo Tutti Insieme*   29

www.brilliantpublications.co.uk

House design sheet

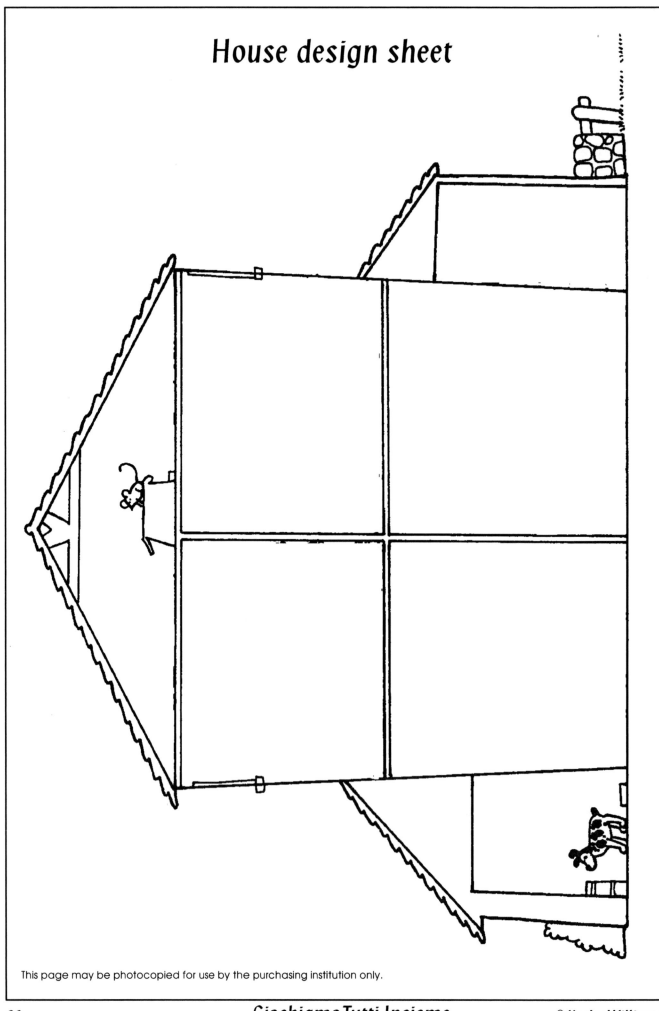

Giochiamo Tutti Insieme

© Kathy Williams

House designers room pictures

Super sporty week

Objectives

- To prompt pupils to use the phrases 'faccio ...', 'vado ...' and 'gioco ...' in conjunction with seven sport activities
- To practise the days of the week (extension activity)

Setting up the game

- Play in pairs or small groups with one game board (page 33) per group.
- Dice and counters are required.
- Each pupil will need a week planner (page 34).

How to play the game

1. Starting at 'Cominciare quì' one pupil throws the die and moves the counter the relevant number of places around the board. They must **say** the phrase indicated by the activity picture on the place where they land. They then write the activity onto a day of their choice on the week planner. The next pupil then takes a turn and so on.
2. Pupils continue to throw the die in turn and move repeatedly around the board, until they have landed on all the activities and chosen which day to write them in. When they land on activities already used they must still say the appropriate sentence.

Parole importanti – Key words

faccio ...	I do ...
il ciclismo	cycling
l'atletica (f)	athletics
vado ...	I go ...
a nuotare	swimming
gioco ...	I play ...
il calcio	football
il rugby	rugby
la palla a canestra	basketball
il tennis	tennis
lunedì	Monday
martedì	Tuesday
mercoledì	Wednesday
giovedì	Thursday
venerdì	Friday
sabato	Saturday
domenica	Sunday

Extensions/variations

- You could make the game competitive by having a time limit, or by having the first player to complete their week as the winner. If you wish all pupils to complete the week plan, encourage those who have finished quickly to listen to and help the others, until all have finished.
- As a follow-up activity pupils could present their weekly activity plans to each other or the class, using for example: 'Lunedì faccio l'atletica. Martedì gioco il calcio.' etc.

Super sporty week board game

Cominciare qui

Giochiamo Tutti Insieme

Super sporty week board game

lunedì	
martedì	
mercoledì	
giovedì	
venerdì	
sabato	
domenica	

This page may be photocopied for use by the purchasing institution only.

Giochiamo Tutti Insieme

Weather reporters

Objectives

- To ask and answer questions about the weather
- To reinforce the names of some principal towns in Italy

Setting up the game

- Pupils play together in pairs with one weather grid (page 36) each and a set of town and weather cards (page 37) per pair.

How to play the game

1. Put the town cards and the weather cards in two piles, face down.
2. Using the weather grids, both players first make a weather prediction for each of their towns and tell them to their partner in Italian. They record their forecasts in writing or by drawing a picture in the 'weather forecast' column on the grid.
3. One player then picks up a town name card and asks what the weather is like there using 'Come fa il tempo a …?' e.g. 'Come fa il tempo a Roma?' The town card used is put to one side.
4. The other player picks a weather card and answers using the weather pictured, e.g. 'A Roma piove.' The cards can be interpreted in a number of possible ways, for example the sun card could be 'È una bella giornata / Ci stà il sole / Fa caldo.' If this is what either player predicted they put a tick in the second column; if they were wrong they put a cross. The weather card used is returned to the bottom of the pile.
5. The players swap roles and continue asking and answering until all the towns' weather conditions have been filled in on the grid.
6. The winner is the player who scored the most ticks at the end of the game.

Weather reporters town grid

Town	Weather forecast	✓ or ✗
Roma		
Firenze		
Milano		
Venezia		
Pisa		
Torino		
Napoli		
Palermo		

Giochiamo Tutti Insieme

Weather reports

✂

Firenze	Roma
Venezia	Milano
Torino	Pisa
Palermo	Napoli

Triple time

Objectives

- To practise telling the time in Italian
- To reinforce understanding of digital and analogue times and the times written out in Italian
- To revise the difference between 'è' and 'sono' when talking about the time. 'È' is used with one o'clock, midday and midnight. 'Sono' is used with all other times, e.g. 'È l'una', 'Sono le due', 'Sono le tre', etc.

Parole importanti – Key words

è/sono …	it is …
l'una	one o'clock
le due	two o'clock
le tre	three o'clock
le quattro	four o'clock
le cinque	five o'clock
le sei	six o'clock
le sette	seven o'clock
le otto	eight o'clock
le nove	nine o'clock
le dieci	ten o'clock
le undici	eleven o'clock
mezzogiorno	midday
mezzanotte	midnight

Setting up the game

- Pupils work in pairs.
- Pupils need one set of time cards from page 39 per pair. You could make more cards to practise other times.

How to play the game

1. In pairs, players have a set of time cards in front of them, face down on the table.
2. One player turns over three different cards, trying to find a matching set of three. If he finds three which all say the same time – in digital, analogue and in Italian – he keeps the set. If the three cards do not match, they are turned face down again and the other player has a turn. (The game works just like a 'pairs' game, except that the players are finding three cards.)
3. To aid the players' chances of finding a match, if they turn over two which match in one go, they keep these to one side until their next turn, when they have three chances to find the third card. If the third card is not found during that turn, they keep the pair to the side until the third is found on a further turn. If their opponent turns over the card that they are missing from their set, this card must be returned to the table, face down.
4. When the players are turning over the cards, encourage them to say the times out loud in Italian every time, using a whole sentence, e.g. 'Sono le cinque.'

Extension/variation

- The times are only on the hour, so that players can concentrate on their Italian. You could make more cards which show half past, quarter to, etc. if you feel that your pupils can manage.

It is half past one.	È l'una e mezzo.
It is quarter past three.	Sono le tre e un quarto.
It is quarter to six.	Sono le sei meno un quarto.

Triple time cards

Sono le tre.	**3:00**	
Sono le nove.	**9:00**	
Sono le undici.	**11:00**	
È mezzogiorno / mezzanotte.	**12:00**	

Set 2

Sono le otto.	**8:00**	
Sono le quattro.	**4:00**	
Sono le due.	**2:00**	
Sono le sei.	**6:00**	

Giochiamo Tutti Insieme

The best/worst day ever at school

Objectives

- To practise saying school subjects
- To practise counting
- To practise saying times on the hour

Setting up the game

- Pupils need a 'school day timetable' (page 41) each and one 'Chinese counter' per pair (page 42). Cut out the grid and fold to make the counter.
- Pupils work in pairs.

How to play the game

1. Players fill in their 'ideal' timetable first in the right-hand column of the school day timetable sheet. They then fold back this column so that they cannot see the subjects they have written.

2. Player one picks a time for a lesson from his/her timetable at random, e.g. 'alle tre'.

3. Player two (who has the 'chinese counter') counts and moves the counter in and out **three** times, counting 'uno, due, tre'.

4. Player one then picks one of the numbers visible on the counter, in Italian, e.g. if five is visible he/she may pick that and say 'cinque'.

5. Player two counts and moves the counter again, this time **five** times.

6. Player one then chooses one of the visible numbers on the counter and this time player two lifts up the corresponding flap.

7. Under the flap is a school subject. Player one reads this out to player two, who then writes this into his/her timetable, in the hour that he/she originally chose (in this case 'alle tre'). Players must say out loud the timetable and subject as they fill this part in, e.g. 'Alle tre ho l'italiano.'

8. The players keep swapping over roles of choosing and counting so that both players can complete their timetables.

9. When all timetables are complete the class reveal and discuss their results. The best or worst school day!

Extension/variation

- The 'Chinese counter' is a very adaptable resource that can be used for counting practice as well as having different vocabulary written inside. For example, instead of school subjects, write in buildings. The day's timetable can be filled in to say the time that each building is visited on a tour of the town. Use 'visito …' instead of 'ho …'

Parole importanti – Key words

l'italiano (m)	Italian
l'arte (f)	art
l'inglese (m)	English
la storia	history
la musica	music
il computer	ICT
la matematica	maths
la scienza	science
ho	I have
a l'una	at one o'clock
alle due	at two o'clock
tre	three
quattro	four
cinque	five
sei	six
sette	seven
otto	eight
nove	nine
dieci	ten
undici	eleven
dodici	twelve

GiochiamoTutti Insieme

School day timetable

	ho …	ho …
alle 9		
alle 10		
alle 11		
a l'1		
alle 2		
alle 3		
alle 4		

Chinese counter template

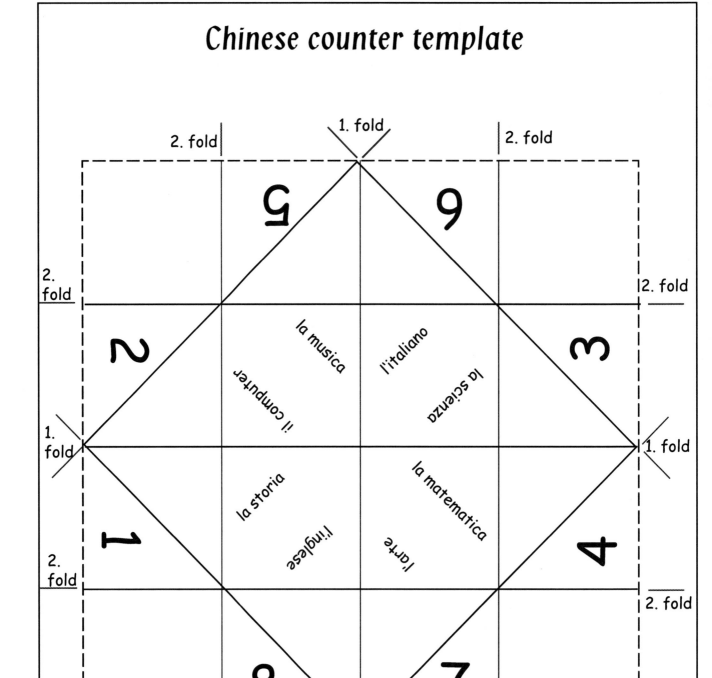

1. Fold corners **back** behind face of paper.
2. Fold corners **inward** to centre.
3. Put your thumb and forefinger of both
   hands into the back of the resulting
   square and pinch up into a point.

Like it or not

Objectives
■ To practise saying 'mi piace ...' and 'non mi piace ...', while talking about school subjects

Setting up the game
■ Pupils play in pairs using an enlarged photocopy of the grid (page 44), a coin, and a different coloured counter each.

How to play the game
1. The players put their counters on 'Cominciare quì'.
2. They decide who goes first by tossing a coin.
3. Player one tosses the coin – if **heads**, player one moves his/her counter to 'Mi piace ...' completing the phrase with a school subject, for example, 'Mi piace la musica.' If **tails**, player one moves to the 'Non mi piace ...' position instead, and completes the phrase accordingly.
4. Player two then tosses the coin and moves/speaks in the same way. Both players can be on the same place on the grid at the same time.
5. They continue to move across the grid until the first player reaches the last column on the right-hand side of the board. Player two must then throw the opposite to player one's last throw, and complete the opposite phrase to avoid losing the game. For example, if player one completed the course by throwing heads and said 'Mi piace ...' then player two has to throw tails to finish, or he has automatically lost the game. If he throws tails then the game is a draw.
6. On completing the game, the players start again (and again) at 'Cominciare quì', with alternating players starting the game. They should keep a tally of how many games they win. They could play 'best of five' for example.
7. By repeating the game (at a quick pace for older pupils) the language is being continually reinforced. You could make it more challenging by saying that players must not repeat a school subject if their partner has already said it within that game. There are ten school subjects listed in the key words list, so this should be possible.

Extension/variation
■ The game can be adapted to practise likes and dislikes of other things, e.g. different foods or sports. Note: when talking about plural things, 'mi piace ...' changes to 'mi piacciono ...', and 'non mi piace ...' to 'non mi piacciono ...', e.g. 'Mi piacciono le mele' (I like apples), 'Non mi piacciono i piselli' (I don't like peas).

Parole importanti – Key words

mi piace ...	I like ...
non mi piace ...	I don't like ...
l'italiano	Italian
l'arte	art
l'educazione fisica	PE
l'inglese	English
la storia	history
la geografia	geography
la musica	music
il computer	ICT
la matematica	maths
la scienza	science

Like it or not coin grid

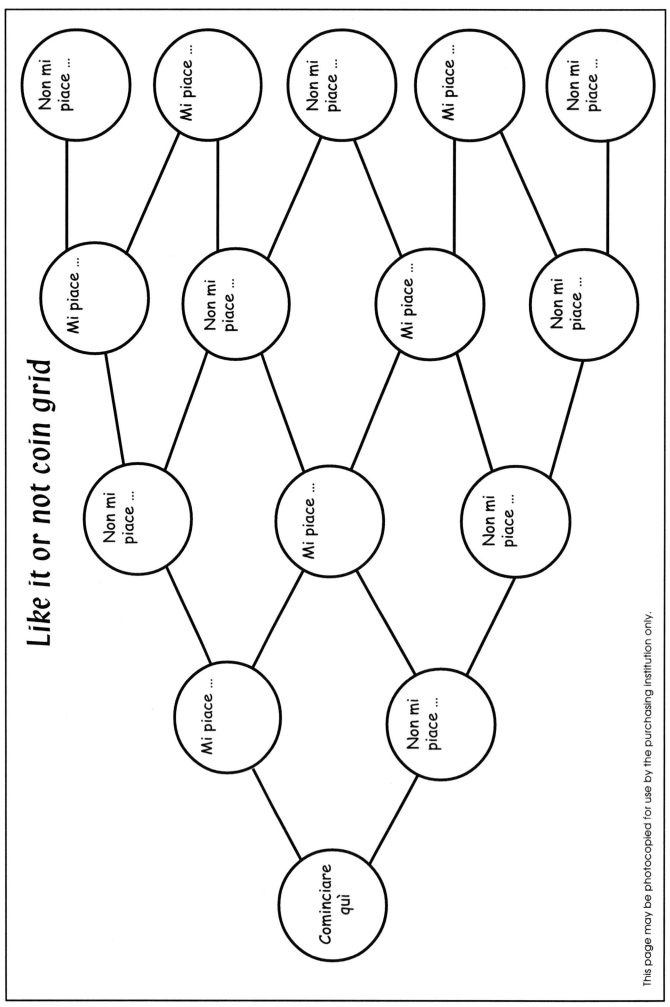

A tour of Italy

Objectives

- To practise using transport words
- To practise using 'Vado a + town'

Setting up the game

- All players require a map (page 47) each and one die between them, made from the template (page 48). This can be coloured and assembled in advance of the game by the players.
- The same game can be played either in pairs or groups of three or four.

Parole importanti – Key words

vado a ...	I am going to ...
Roma, Firenze, Torino, etc.	
in corriera, con la corriera	by bus
in barca / nave, con la barca / nave	by boat
in macchina, con la macchina	by car
in aeroplano, con l'aeroplano	by plane
in treno, con il treno	by train
con bicicletta	by bike

How to play the game

1. Make sure all the players can identify the names of the main towns featured on the map before the game begins.
2. Each player must make a round trip of Italy, from Rome back to Rome, via the route shown on the map.
3. The players must keep their maps hidden from the view of the other player(s). This is because in the final part of the game, points are lost if two players have chosen the same form of transport for the same leg of the tour.
4. One player starts by rolling the die. He must say aloud the form of transport that he throws, and then quietly decide which part of the route he will make using that form of transport. It can be any leg of the journey that is chosen. For example, if he threw a train picture, he could decide to travel by train between Florence (Firenze) and Turin (Torino). He makes a note of his choice in the itinerary table below the map, and writes down the points he has scored using the die. Take care to fill in the correct line on the points tally.
5. The next player then throws the die, and makes a choice on his travel itinerary in the same way. The game continues until each player has made a complete route around Italy. They might have thrown the same picture most of the time and made almost the whole route by car, for example. Or they may have a wide variety of modes of transport in their travel itinerary. If, however, the boat is thrown, it can only be used between Naples (Napoli) and Palermo, or Palermo and Rome. If they throw a boat and these legs of the journey have already been filled in, they have to miss a turn. Pupils can still use the bus, car, train or bike for the legs to and from Palermo, because it is possible to travel by road or rail for the majority of the journey and take the ferry across the 5km of water separating Sicily from the mainland. You can explain this to them if they ask. (If they do this, they do not need to assign the boat for the ferry crossing as well.)

To score points

■ Player one starts by saying in Italian one of the sections of his journey, for example, 'Vado a Venezia in macchina.' The other player(s) look(s) at their maps, and if they have used the car for this section as well, then they all lose their points for this section. If only the first player has used the car here then he keeps his 1 point (on the die the car is worth 1 point).

■ The next player then says one of her sections, 'Vado a Napoli con il treno.' The other players check their maps and either cross off their train and points, or leave other transport choices in place. As before, the player speaking only keeps her points if she is the only player to use the train in this part of the tour.

■ When the whole route has been discussed, the winner is the player with the most points.

Giochiamo Tutti Insieme   © *Kathy Williams*

A tour of Italy

Londra

Milano   Venezia

Torino

Firenze

Roma

Napoli

Palermo

Vado a Roma	...........in aeroplano............	_4_	points
Vado a Firenze	....	_____	points
Vado a Torino	....	_____	points
Vado a Milano	....	_____	points
Vado a Venezia	....	_____	points
Vado a Napoli	....	_____	points
Vado a Palermo	....	_____	points
Vado a Roma	....	_____	points

Die template for a tour of Italy

Giochiamo Tutti Insieme

© Kathy Williams

Quiz corners

Objective
- To assess pupils' knowledge of several areas of language or vocabulary as a 'round-up' of a few weeks' work. The teacher can monitor answers orally during the game, or answers can be written down for the whole class to check at the end of the session.

Setting up the game
- In this game the questions can be in English so that the emphasis is on producing the right language in response, rather than trying to understand the question. Alternatively, as pupils become more knowledgable and confident, both questions and answers can be in Italian.
- Photocopy and cut out the question vocabulary cards (page 50). Fill in the blanks to practise the particular area(s) of vocabulary that you want to assess. Alternatively, pupils could prepare these in advance for others in the class to use. If you play with just one set of cards, the pupils will have to return them so that other pairs/groups can also answer those questions. Alternatively, if you prepare several sets of cards, pupils could keep the cards and write their answers on them.
- Pupils work in pairs or small groups.

How to play the game
1. Designate the four corners of the classroom as the four 'quiz corners' (or if this is not feasible, four table tops, four trays or boxes). Using four separate areas makes it more interesting than a 'sit-down' test as pupils have to move between the areas and their 'bases'.
2. Name each corner with the first four letters of the Italian alphabet.
3. Place an equal amount of cards in each of the four corners.
4. Player one chooses a corner at random. Player two has to pick up a card from there and ask player one the question written on the card. Player two then returns the card to the bottom of the pile he/she took it from (if you are playing with just one set of cards).
5. It is now the turn of player two to pick a corner, from which player one has to pick up a question card.
6. If the card chosen has already been answered, the players must still answer the question again before continuing. The fact that some cards may be repeatedly picked up in the attempt to find them all is beneficial as it gives pupils extra practice through repetition.
7. The game can be made competitive by setting a time limit within which the pair/group answering the most questions correctly wins. Alternatively the winning pair/group is the one which completes all the questions first.

Extension/variation
- Each corner could be used to practise a different theme, for example, weather in the 'A' corner, classroom items in the 'B' corner, days of the week in the 'C' corner, etc. Alternatively all the areas could have the same theme.

Corner question vocabulary cards

1. What is _____ in Italian?	2. What is _____ in Italian?	3. What is _____ in Italian?
4. What is _____ in Italian?	5. What is _____ in Italian?	6. What is _____ in Italian?
7. What is _____ in Italian?	8. What is _____ in Italian?	9. What is _____ in Italian?
10. What is _____ in Italian?	11. What is _____ in Italian?	12. What is _____ in Italian?

Giochiamo Tutti Insieme

Rock, paper, scissors

Objective

■ To test vocabulary or spelling using the 'rock, paper, scissors' hand game – more fun than writing down answers to a list of questions! (It can be used to practise any language area.)

Parole importanti – Key words

roccia (f)	rock
carta (f)	paper
forbici (f, pl)	scissors

Setting up the game

■ You can use the cards from 'quiz corners' (page 50) and the spelling cards (page 52). You will need two types of questions – ones which ask for an **oral response**, e.g. 'What is the Italian word for "cheese"?' and ones which ask the players to **spell** a word, e.g. 'Spell the word for "cheese" in Italian'. Alternatively questions can be in Italian, e.g. 'Come si dice "cheese" in italiano?' or 'Come si scrive "cheese" in italiano?'

■ Players sit in pairs around a table with the question cards in two piles in the middle. They need paper to record scores and for written responses.

How to play the game

1. On the count of three in Italian they each put out one hand, with the hand made into one of three shapes – **rock** which is the fist clenched into a ball shape, **paper** which is a flat hand palm downwards, or **scissors** which is the forefinger and middle finger opening and closing (like scissors). If you wish, you could use the Italian words for 'rock, paper, scissors' (see key words).

2. A player wins the round in the following ways:
   ■ 'paper' beats 'rock'
   ■ 'rock' beats 'scissors'
   ■ 'scissors' beats 'paper'

3. If both players have chosen the same hand shape, then there is no winner for that round and they must play again.

4. Whoever wins a round answers a question.
   ■ If he won using 'paper', his opponent asks him to **write down** a word.
   ■ If he won using 'rock', he has to **answer a question orally**.
   ■ If he won using 'scissors' he can cut his opponent's score back by one point, or he can opt for a question that his opponent chooses.

5. Answering questions correctly will get 2 points, incorrectly 0 points.

6. The winner is the player who has the most points at the end of a time limit, or when all the questions have been used up, whichever is most suitable.

Extension/variation

■ Without using written question cards or point scoring, this game works well as a warm-up, a way of players testing each other orally on any subject they wish. It also works well as a time filler at the end of a lesson. Players do the 'rock, paper, scissors' actions and the winner answers questions as before, but they could be anything thought up by their partner, or from a particular theme or vocabulary list.

Spelling cards

1. How do you spell _____ in Italian?	**2.** How do you spell _____ in Italian?	**3.** How do you spell _____ in Italian?
4. How do you spell _____ in Italian?	**5.** How do you spell _____ in Italian?	**6.** How do you spell _____ in Italian?
7. How do you spell _____ in Italian?	**8.** How do you spell _____ in Italian?	**9.** How do you spell _____ in Italian?
10. How do you spell _____ in Italian?	**11.** How do you spell _____ in Italian?	**12.** How do you spell _____ in Italian?

Giochiamo Tutti Insieme

Also available from Brilliant Publications

C'est Français!   ISBN: 978-1-903853-02-3
A Photocopiable French Scheme for Primary Schools
A book and supporting CD with over 60 photocopiable pupil sheets to provide
practice and reinforcement through simple, fun exercises. 18 thematic units cover
themes ranging from 'Holidays' and 'The days of the week' to 'Clothes' and 'My
town'. Each unit has a clearly laid out lesson plan, key word list, learning
objectives, resources needed, suggested classroom activities and further activities
to extend learning.

¡Es Español!   ISBN: 978-1-903853-64-1
A Photocopiable Spanish Scheme for Primary Schools
A book and supporting CD with over 60 photocopiable pupil sheets to provide
practice and reinforcement through simple, fun exercises. 18 thematic units cover
themes ranging from 'Weather' and 'Animals' to 'Food' and 'Sports'. Each unit has
a clearly laid out lesson plan, key word list, learning objectives, resources needed,
suggested classroom activities and further activities to extend learning.

Chantez Plus Fort!   ISBN: 978-1-903853-37-5
20 Photocopiable Easy–to–Learn French Songs for Primary Schools
20 songs to introduce and reinforce vocabulary for topics such as 'greetings',
'numbers', 'classroom instructions', 'rhymes and sounds', and 'weather'.
Teacher's notes give ideas on how to introduce, use and extend the songs.

The fully photocopiable book comes in a set with 2 CDs. CD 1 contains the 20
songs (16 original, 4 traditional) sung by French children and 13 mini dialogues.
CD 2 contains instrumental tracks for the 16 original songs so you can see how well
your pupils are progressing.

100+ Fun Ideas for Practising   ISBN: 978-1-903853-98-6
Modern Foreign Languages in the Primary Classroom
137 tried and tested activities to develop oracy and literacy skills in almost any
language. Sue Cave, the author has chosen these particular ideas due to the
positive impact the games and activities have had in her classroom.

Jouons Tous Ensemble   ISBN: 978-1-903853-81-8
20 games to play with children to encourage and reinforce French language and
vocabulary.

Juguemos Todos Juntos   ISBN: 978-1-903853-95-5
20 games to play with children to encourage and reinforce Spanish language and
vocabulary.

Wir Spielen Zusammen   ISBN: 978-1-903853-97-9
20 games to play with children to encourage and reinforce German language
and vocabulary.

Brilliant Publications   sales: 01202 712910   website: www.brilliantpublications.co.uk

Printed in the United Kingdom by
Lightning Source UK Ltd., Milton Keynes
137638UK00001B/27-126/A